A Quick and Easy Guide for Genealogists

Researching the Plain Religions

Stephanie Pitcher Fishman

Rebecca Hills
Books

Researching the Plain Religions by Stephanie Pitcher Fishman
Published by Rebecca Hills Books
Part of the Quick & Easy Guides for Genealogists series

Cover graphics came from the following photographers under the Compfight's Creative Commons license:
Amish Hats: Jakob Christensen
Amish Farm Kids: Ian Lamont
Amish, Lancaster County: Franco Folini
Amish Buggy Ride: Anita Ritenour

Thank you for purchasing this Quick & Easy Guide for Genealogists. Please consider leaving a review on the page that you purchased this book. By reviewing it and telling others, you will help me share this work with other family historians. I greatly appreciate your support!

Please visit the author's website at
www.stephaniefishman.com.

For those who've gone before us...

Researching the Plain Religions

Table of Contents

Introduction to Plain Religions

R eligions in America vary from structured to relaxed; historical to new age. Included in this country's social history are those sects commonly called the "plain religions." Plain religions, also called Plain People, are described as being Christian religious sects within the Anabaptist group that follow practices of simple living, separation from the world, and plain dress. Examples of plain religions include Amish and Mennonite, Huguenots, Hutterites, and Shakers. Though each are researched following standard practices for church records, it is helpful to know how each community is structured so that the correct records can be located.

This guide will give you the basics of records, research, and terminology for each religious sect. Each section will also include helpful resources such as brief time lines, information on migration patterns, and of course research links to get you started both on-line and off. I've described the reasons that I find each website helpful in order to save you some time; however, I encourage you to check them out for yourselves. You'll be surprised how many times the records or histories of another denomination appears side by side with one you'd never expect. Don't limit yourself to one section. Flip through each to see if there is a possible tie in to the church your ancestor called home.

*Note: The Amish and Mennonite religions

will be studied together due to their similarities.

How to Get Started

C hurch records are just like any other record set. You must first place your ancestor on the map in order to locate the area in which to begin your search. Consider their country of origin, your present religious affiliation, or the churches available to them in their area. If you've identified the denomination of your ancestors as a "plain" religion, take the time to become familiar with the history of the church if it is unknown to you. Some closed communities are inherently more difficult to access, so you your research may be best served by joining a society or association intended for the preservation of the history and culture of your ancestor's faith.

One thing to remember as you start learning more about your ancestors who practice plain religions is that your experiences with church records may help you in this research. Or it may not. It all depends on the religion. You need to take a look at how the church is organized so that you understand the record types they created.

History and culture will be a big focus for you if you are wanting to go beyond finding a transcription on-line. Each church has its own structure, and many times it is connected to the old country or the culture of the first immigrants into America. Old order churches are still in existence, and their culture can be much different than typical America. It's very important to understand the structure of the church at the time of your ancestors so that you know where to look, what to expect, and how to locate the records.

Some religions will not allow the general public to have access to their records. In this case, genealogical, lineage, and historical societies will be a key to your success. There are several active societies associated with these religions that we'll discuss later.

Just like today, our ancestors left their churches. They moved memberships. They changed denominations. Geography can really be your friend if you suspect that you have a plain religion in your family.

Take a look at the community in which they lived, and start working your way out. Some plain religions dictated where your ancestors worshiped based on where they lived.

Also, look at their country of origin.

Immigrants tended to find churches from or related to their churches back home just like today.

Migration patterns can also help you determine a connection to a plain religion. For example, many areas actually enacted anti-Quaker laws which forced members of this church to move several times. This created very distinct migration patterns. Look at migration patterns for the area and compare them to your family's movements. You may see that they followed the same pattern that many Quaker or Hutterite families took which could indicate a possible clue to their church affiliation.

PART ONE: THE AMISH & MENNONITES

Introduction to
The Amish & Mennonites

L et's talk about the Amish and Mennonites! Why are we talking about them together? Because the Amish sect was originally part of the Mennonite church until a split occurred because the Amish church split in favor of a stricter lifestyle and Biblical interpretation. Their records are similar and will use a lot of the same structure and terminology. And, because the Amish originally split from the Mennonite church, you may find information on both religions in books and websites as you research. It will help you to understand both communities.

Originally, Mennonites were known as Anabaptists. Today, this refers to a wide number of Protestant faiths that agree on the same basic principles: no infant baptism, baptism of believers only, and common social and economic beliefs. They are also similar in their beginnings, having all been established after the early to mid-1500s. Mennonites are a predominate faith in the Anabaptist group.

In 1693, Mennonite immigrants began arriving in the United States. Ten short years later, a split in the church created two distinct sects and the Amish church was born. The Amish live in a stricter fashion with specific mandates on life within the community, the home, and the church than Mennonite families. For example, marriage to non-Amish is strictly prohibited, as is divorce.

Records

Because infant baptism is not used in the Amish and Mennonite churches, you will not find this type of information to provide birth information. Typical marriage documents may not be located. However, there may be mentions in the news and records of the day celebrating the event. Look for family sources. Early records may not be in English, and Amish records may contain words, terms, phrases, or complete records in Pennsylvania Dutch. If you are researching at a repository, don't be afraid to ask for help from the librarians and archivists.

The newsletters, magazines, and other historical publications listed in the **On-line Research** section could hold the key to your ancestors' story. Be sure to look through them for your surnames as well as historical information for the area where they lived.

A concise overview of the Mennonite record structure and FHL holdings can be found on the FamilySearch Wiki[1]. This will also give you a good overview of the records you may find for your Amish ancestors as well.

An interesting fact about marriages: Weddings are typically held in November as winters bring questionable weather, spring brings planting, and fall brings harvest.

Church Structure

The Mennonite and Amish churches are similar in their use of bishops, elders, and deacons within each local congregation. Typically, their local church comes together based on proximity so everyone can travel easily.

Mennonite Church Structure: There are several divisions within the Mennonite faith, including the Mennonite Church (sometimes called the Old Mennonite Church), the General Conference Mennonite Church, and the Mennonite Brethren Church. Each congregation chooses its own governing body through casting of lots for bishop, elders, and deacons.

Amish Church Structure: The local church uses bishops, ministers, and deacons. Churches are organized in districts with approximately 100–150 members in each district. Old Order congregations are smaller in number and are stricter than other Amish congregations.

Research Tips

- Don't get frustrated.

- Look for events around November. Such as Marriage – many times weddings would occur at times that were less busy with the farm. Not spring around planting or fall around harvest.

- Society journals and newspapers will give you a lot of good information on families and communities. Reach out to your repositories and historical societies.

Time Line:
The Amish & Mennonites

1536: Dutch priest Menno Simmons left the Catholic Church in support of the Anabaptist movement.

1683: Mennonites began arriving in Pennsylvania.

1693: Split between Amish and Mennonite churches due to the Amish desire for a stricter lifestyle.

1710: The Swiss Mennonite migration began. Most settled in Lancaster County, Pennsylvania.

1725: The Mennonite church adopted the Dordrecht Confession as their statement of faith.

1812: The Reformed Mennonites were formed in Lancaster County, Pennsylvania by John Herr.

1860: The General Conference Mennonite Church was formed.

1872: The Old Order (Wisler) Mennonite Church was formed by Jacob Wisler, Indiana Mennonite bishop, in protest to using English during services.

Migration Patterns: The Amish & Mennonites

L ike many other faiths, the initial migration waves of the Amish and Mennonite ancestors began with the search for relief from persecution. You'll find the largest numbers of people relocating from Europe to America first at the end of the 1600s and beginning of the 1700s.

Although Pennsylvania had several popular areas, Lancaster County saw the most growth in Mennonite and later Amish communities. These churches didn't stay in Pennsylvania, however. They moved across the area into the states of Ohio and Indiana as well as north into Canada. While these areas are still home to the largest concentration of Amish and Mennonite settlements, several other Midwestern and Mid-Atlantic states have become home as well. If you can't find your family after a move, look for your ancestors in states such as Iowa, Missouri, Michigan, and, to a lesser extent, New York.

A Quick Overview of Major Migration Patterns

- **1683:** The first major wave of migrations from Europe into America, mostly into Pennsylvania.
- **1710:** A second major wave of migrations bringing families from Switzerland into

Pennsylvania.

- **1800s:** Migrations from Pennsylvania into Ohio, Indiana, and Canada (mostly Ontario.)

Locations of Current Colonies

- States with major communities include: Ohio, Pennsylvania, Indiana, Wisconsin, New York, Michigan.
- Other states with several thousand or fewer (according to the 2010 U.S. Religious Census) are scattered throughout the Midwest and New England.
- Canada

Terminology:
The Amish & Mennonites

As you research your family's history, you may notice that many of the terms used will not be in English. You'll encounter variations on German dialects such as Pennsylvania Dutch. Search out a genealogy society or library in the area of your research for help. Lean on your societies and librarians for help. You may encounter Pennsylvania Dutch, German, or other variations.

Basic Terminology

Ordnung: Written and unwritten rules for Amish life.

Streng Meidung: shunning; casting out and avoiding of an Amish church member who is not living according to church beliefs and mandates.

Old Order Amish: A strict form of Amish faith, this church body uses bishops, ministers, and deacons. Though still in existence, the number of Old Order Amish is smaller. Churches are organized in districts with approximately 100 – 150 members in each district.

Major Repositories: The Amish & Mennonites

W hen you dive into your research, you'll notice one thing: all of these repositories are Mennonite repositories. Because it was the predominant Anabaptist faith, the Mennonite church is among the largest and is therefore the cornerstone sect if one exists. In many of these repositories, you'll find information and records pertaining to your Anabaptist, Amish, and Hutterite ancestors as well.

Repositories

Mennonite Church US Archives[2]

This is the official archive of the Mennonite church. The website includes finding aids, digitized photographs, search capabilities, and more. You can also search their partner site: MennObits[3].

Mennonite Historical Library[4]

This archive is one of the most comprehensive archives in the country for this particular type of research. They have a wide variety of records and information pertaining to not only the Mennonite church but also the Amish, the Hutterites, and others in the Anabaptist movement.

Lancaster Mennonite
Historical Society Library[5]

The LMHS has several on-line databases that are free to research, including obituary indexes, property indexes, and cemetery listings. However, the real excitement comes with the member databases. Membership fees are reasonable. If you are considering it but would like to know first if it is a good fit for your research, contact their staff with questions.

Menno Simons Historical Library[6]

Not only do they house a large number of Mennonite records and histories, the Menno Simons Historical Library also includes records on other Anabaptist and Shenandoah Valley ancestors. The website also contains interesting links and resources, including audio clips.

Mennonite Historical Collections
Bluffton University[7]

Housed in a new Special Collections floor, this library includes two special collections: The Mennonite Collection and the Genealogy Collection. Materials are available during appointments only, however there are some on-line search options and other research resources available.

On-line Research: The Amish & Mennonites

Websites

Cyndi's List: Mennonite[8] & Cyndi's List: Amish[9]

Amish & Mennonite resources at one of the genealogy community's foremost websites.

Amish and Plain People[10]

This website has an easy-to-read history of the Amish and Plain People of Lancaster County, Pennsylvania, as well as some additional articles that may be of interest as you learn about the lives your ancestors may have lived.

Kindred Trails:

Amish, Mennonite, & Anabaptist Genealogy & Family History Resources[11]

This page of Kindred Trails includes links to many on-line record sets and histories. (Be sure to check out the other religions listed in the right sidebar!)

Amish America:

Exploring Amish Culture and Communities[12]

My favorite part of this website is the blog. Read through for posts on history-related topics such as the Amish in War, or search the genealogy tag for posts related to family history. Check out the other fun parts of the site, like peeks inside Amish businesses and homes of today.

Swiss Anabaptist Genealogical Association[13]

Consider joining this genealogical society if your ancestors are of Swiss Anabaptist descent. The website isn't fancy, but their links section is very helpful and their membership dues are extremely affordable.

Mennonite DNA Project[14]

Interested in joining a DNA project? This project through Family Tree DNA encompasses results from Amish, Mennonite, Old Order, and Hutterite descents as well as other Anabaptist religions.

Global Anabaptist Mennonite Encyclopedia On-line[15]

Do you have a question about Mennonites? Look here.

MennObits[16]

A collection of Amish and Mennonite obituaries from 1864 on. Part of the Historical Committee of the Mennonite Church.

Mennonite Family History Quarterly[17]

For those that like genealogy magazines, this quarterly publication includes sections on surnames, queries, books for sale, family tries, and more.

Mennonite Historian[18]

This publication's genealogy column will be especially useful if you have Canadian ancestors. Current subscriptions are available, and the site also includes a free PDF archive of past issues.

The Mennonite Quarterly Review[19]

This quarterly publication has been printed since 1927. New subscriptions are available. Indexes of past issues are available from 1997 forward.

Mennonite Ship List 1872-1904[20]

Although this is a plain text page, it has a massive amount of names listed. The original compiler is also listed if you would like to contact them as well.

Webcast: Amish Resources at the Library of Congress[21]

This is a great video explaining the resources available to you in the Library of Congress collections.

North Dakota State University Library: Mennonite Dialect, Genealogy, and History[22]

This list of links includes historical societies, dictionaries, biographical indexes, and more.

Facebook Groups

Mennonite Genealogy & History[23]

Connect with others researching their Mennonite ancestors.

Amish Q&A[24]

Do you have questions about the Amish community? Ask them here.

Message Boards

- **Amish Message Board**[25] on Ancestry.com
- **Volhynian-Mennonite Message Board**[26] on Ancestry.com
- **Prussian-Russian Mennonites Message Board**[27] on Ancestry.com

PART TWO: THE HUGUENOTS

Introduction to
The Huguenots

T he Huguenots were members of the French Reformed Church, a group of protestant Christians following John Calvin who faced fierce persecution from the Catholic Church. They sought refuge in countries such as Holland, Germany, Switzerland, England, Ireland, and the United States (then the British colonies.) Within this group, you'll be looking at records that are generally in the 16th and 17th centuries, although you will find some records into the 1700s and early 1800s.

Huguenots settling in New England, primarily New York, generally joined the Dutch church. Those settling in the southern colonies, primarily in South Carolina, generally joined the Anglican Church. Church registers will include information on baptisms and marriages. Deaths will most likely be recorded separately, though funerals may not be included. Burials will rarely be found.

If you have French ancestry this may be very applicable to your research. Be cautious that you don't assume your surname means that you are of Huguenot descent. Tread carefully, and explore the many histories available in public and private libraries.

French names were easily Americanized in many ways. Your names may vary in spelling even within a family. Don't get hung up on looking for an exact spelling. Lean heavily on mapping your ancestors to see if closely spelled names appear together during migrations.

Look for societies and libraries in the country that your ancestors sought refuge. For American records, look for repositories to be concentrated in New York, Pennsylvania, and South Carolina.

Church Structure

- Roles and positions in the church will be similar to other Reformed, Protestant churches
- Terms will be similar to other Christian denominations, though typically written in French

Records

There aren't too many surprises with the structure of a Huguenot church. They will be very similar to the records that you'll find in other Protestant churches, however they will most likely be recorded in French. You'll find birth, marriage, and death records within the church documents, though burials were rarely recorded.

Translations and transcriptions of some records are available on-line, and you may be able to find records in both historical society libraries and public libraries alike. For example, the main branch of the Columbus Metropolitan Library in Columbus, Ohio, holds a large collection of Huguenot records in their genealogy and local history department. Your largest barriers in locating your ancestors in documents will be the language and the age of the records.

Many times, the Huguenot church merged with other churches in the area. You may want to check the following church records for your surnames as well: Dutch Reformed, Presbyterian, Episcopal, Reformed, Congregational, and Anglican.

Societies are going to be very important in this research simply because of the language barrier and the migration to other countries before settling in what would become the United States. Many societies exist, and many hold the largest record sets. Look for societies in the various countries to which they may have emigrated.

Research Tips

- Names: However, there are many sources on-line that hold listings of surnames associated with the church. Very fun to look through!

- Don't get hung up on names. French names are Anglicized, and not all French ancestors were Huguenots.
- Find a society! Check out the National Huguenot Society.[28]

Time Line:
The Huguenots

1533: John Calvin leaves Paris.

1536: An edict is issued for extermination of "heretics" – the Huguenots.

1560: Huguenots call for an end to the persecution and threaten revolt.

1562: French religious wars begin.

1585: Huguenots expelled from France.

1598: Edict of Nantes provides protection for Huguenots in France.

1621: Huguenots start arriving in New York along the Hudson River.

1629: Huguenots migrate to Virginia.

1662: Huguenots arrive in Massachusetts.

1667: A Huguenot colony settles in Hackensack, Bergen County, New Jersey.

1679: Huguenots arrive in South Carolina.

1685: Louis XIV revokes the Edict of Nantes which

results in another wave of persecution and fleeing from France.

1721: Huguenots settle in Connecticut.

1752: Huguenots settle in Maine.

Migration Patterns: The Huguenots

As the French Protestant church of the day, the Huguenots faced periods of both great persecution and great acceptance in France. In the two short years between 1559 and 1561, over two thousand Huguenot churches were in use. The acceptance, however, did not last long before religious wars broke out across the country. During several of these, families fled to non-Catholic areas, including eventually the United States. Although the path through Europe and then to the New World will be what most trace their ancestors along, it is wise to note that another group migrated from Europe into South Africa.

A Quick Overview of Major Migration Patterns

- **Mid 1500s:** The first migration took families from the religious wars of France into non-Catholic areas of Europe (Switzerland, Netherlands, Prussia, etc.)

- **1562:** A colony is established in Florida, though the Spanish push them out of the area within two years.

- **1620s:** Three congregations are established in the Hudson River areas of New York; Shortly after, movement from New York to Virginia begins.

- **1660s:** Huguenot colonies in Virginia begin to head north again into Massachusetts while some of the New York congregations expand into New Jersey.

- **1679:** Settlement in South Carolina is created

- **1700s:** Settlements in Maine and Connecticut are created.

Locations of Current Colonies

- Several churches remain active today, particularly in South Carolina.

- Search for "French Protestant" or "French Huguenot" congregations.

Terminology:
The Huguenots

T erms used in church registers will be written in French. The most comprehensive – and free – resource for Huguenot terminology can be found in PDF form from The Huguenot Society of Great Britain and Ireland: Glossary of French Terms with Examples of Huguenot Register Entries.[29]

Basic Terminology

Ancien: elder

Baptise par: baptized by

Maries par: married by

Ministre: minster

Pasteur: pastor

Temoin: witness

Major Repositories: The Huguenots

U nlike some other, larger religious sects, there is no one official repository of Huguenot records. Historical societies, lineage societies, and regional Huguenot societies will each contain their own unique holdings. Once you've traced your ancestors to a specific location, spend some time looking at the local historical society as well as public and university libraries. You may be surprised what you find!

Repositories

The Historic Huguenot Street[30]

This historical site includes collections and manuscripts related to family history and church information on those who settled in New Paltz, New York and surrounding areas. Through a partnership with Hudson River Valley Heritage, many collections are available online. If you are in the area, however, schedule a visit to tour the living history museum.

Columbus (Ohio) Metropolitan Library: Local History & Genealogy Department[31]

This public library located in downtown Columbus, Ohio, holds a large collection of records related to your Huguenot ancestors.

Call the department's librarian for information on the specific holdings.

The Historical Society of Pennsylvania[32]

This state historical society holds the records of the Huguenot Society of Pennsylvania from 1918 to 2000.

The Huguenot Society of America[33]

Located in New York, this society library holds a wealth of information. However, none of the collections are online. Visits are by appointment only.

On-line Research: The Huguenots

Websites

Cyndi's List: Huguenots[34]

Find a diverse list of links related to the Huguenot church and history.

Genealogy Forum:
Huguenot Reading List[35]

A long and in-depth bibliography of books for the Huguenot researcher.

The Huguenot Society of
Great Britain and Ireland[36]

In addition to a vast collection of educational materials and articles relating to Huguenot history, this society includes a family history section with resources such as how-to guides, French terms, FAQs, and information on other European libraries with information you may find helpful.

The National Huguenot Society[37]

This society provides information, resources,

events, scholarships and more to its members and guests alike.

Huguenot Foundation of South Africa[38]

This organization encompasses the main society, museum, and monument to Huguenots in South Africa.

Facebook Groups

Descendants of the Huguenot Colonists[39]

Are you a descendant? This is a group for you!

Huguenot Heritage[40]

This is a great group for those interested in the history and faith of the Huguenots.

Message Boards

- **Huguenot - Walloons - Europe**[41] on Ancestry.com

PART FOUR: THE SHAKERS

Introduction to
The Shakers

T he name "Shaker" stems from the label that many gave the group, the Shaking Quakers, based on the shaking, dancing, and movement common in their worship services. Because the dances would later become very distinct and intricate, many people would travel to watch the Shakers dance.

The Shaker religion grew from the United Society of Believers in the Second Appearing of Christ during the 1700s. Their beliefs stemmed from the idea that there is a male and female counterpart to everything. Ann Lee, later called Mother Ann, was seen as the female counterpart to Christ and became the leader of the church. In all, nineteen Shaker communities were established in New York, throughout New England, Kentucky, Ohio, and Indiana.

Due to the strictly held beliefs that included a vow of celibacy, the ending of ties outside the church, and the removal of marriage from the typical life events, cha`nces are you aren't going to find whole families leaving for the Shaker community or church. You'll most likely find individuals that, unfortunately, become the end of their branch in your family tree unless they chose to leave the village in which they lived.

Church Structure

The Central Ministry in Mount Lebanon, New York was the main governing body of the Shaker religion. There, two elders and eldresses coordinated and oversaw the Shaker communities within the United States. The body of communities were further divided into bishoprics; groups of closely located communities. These were overseen by two elders and eldresses who would both care for the communities and coordinate communication between the Central Ministry and the local community.

Each local community was made up of two or more communal groups, or "families", led by two elders and eldresses. Each family was led by a pair of deacons and deaconesses who oversaw the daily life of the family as well as two trustees who were responsible for the legal and business goings of the family.

When a person joins the Shaker religion, ties to their families are severed. They are assigned to one of three "families" within the congregation, including names such as Mill, Center, or East. Each family acted as its own entity within the community and held leadership positions in both male and female roles to enforce the gender equality they held as a basic belief within their religious doctrine.

So, the structure goes:

- Individual in a family;
- one deacon and one deaconess over each family along with one trustee over each family;
- one elder and one eldress over the community;

- and a bishopric over several communities in close proximity,

- And over all this is the Central Ministry in Mount Lebanon, New York.

Records

The record sets you'll find for your Shaker ancestors will be different. Remember that they didn't marry or have families of their own outside their communal families, so you won't find these typical vital records. However, some libraries and archives may hold congregational records such as membership records and testimonials.

Try to locate the community in which your Shaker ancestor lived and determine if there is a library or museum in the area. Records of most value are photograph collections, manuscript collections, diaries and journals, and correspondence. Many libraries contain scrapbooks created by members of the Shaker community represented there.

Social history will be the key to understanding your ancestors. Biographies and histories, diaries and journals, even furniture and fiber arts will give you a picture of the type of individual your ancestor was if you can locate them.

Research Tips

- Try to locate your ancestor's community.
- Look for a society, library, or community museum in the area.
- Search manuscript collections at libraries (including university libraries!).
- Don't forget sources like newspapers. Many Shaker communities had newsletters and papers.

Time Line:
The Shakers

1736: Ann Lee is born in Manchester, England.

1747: The United Society of Believers in Christ's Second Appearing was founded in Manchester, England.

1774: Following persecution, Mother Ann led a small group of church members to America settling first in

New York and then throughout New England.

1784: Mother Ann passes away. Father James Whittaker takes over leadership.

1785: The first Shaker worship building is built in Harvard, Massachusetts.

1787: The first Shaker community is established in New Lebanon, New York. Father James passes away.

Mid 1800s: The peak of the Shaker growth

1890s: The Shaker communities begin to close.

Migration Patterns: The Shakers

A small and fledgling religion, the Shakers had smaller migrations than other churches. The main migrations were between the various locations of villages in the United States as missionaries established communities. At the height of the religion, nineteen locations were established.

A Quick Overview of Major Migration Patterns

- 1774: After her release from jail, Anne Lee and her husband move from England to New York.

- 1785: The first Shaker building is raised in Harvard, Massachusetts.

- 1787: The first Shaker community is established in New Lebanon, New York.

- 1805: Missionaries travel from New York to Kentucky.

- Mid-1800s: Shakers move from Kentucky into Indiana and Ohio; from New York throughout New England.

- 1890: Shaker communities begin to close.

Locations of Current Colonies

- In 1989, twelve Shaker followers were recorded.
- Today, many Shaker villages have been restored as living history sites and museums.

Terminology: The Shakers

E ach position within the Shaker church will have a male and female counterpart. Look for names that are similar yet reflect the sex of the person. Example: Deacon and Deaconess.

Basic Terminology

Bishoprics: A group of several Shaker communities close in geographical location.

Central Ministry: The head of the Shaker church government located in Mount Lebanon, New York.

Deacons/Deaconess: The male and female counterparts that oversaw the daily life of the families within a community. Each family had their own deacons and deaconesses, so multiple would be found within a community.

Elders/Eldresses: The male and female counterparts that oversaw a smaller community. Example: The elders/eldresses of Central Ministry oversaw the bishoprics. The elders and eldresses of the bishopric oversaw the communities.

Family: A smaller communal group within a

Shaker community.

Trustees: The male and female counterparts that oversaw the financial and business activities of the family. Each family had their own trustees, so multiple would be found within a community.

Major Repositories: The Shakers

U nlike other religions, the Shaker church did not encourage marriage or the birth of children. Most of the collections within a repository's holdings will be focused on the daily life and art of the Shaker community. You will find a great variety of photographs, poetry, manuscripts, and ephemera related to this sect. Remember your social history! Look for the stories and you will find them.

Repositories

Shaker Library at
Sabbathday Lake Shaker Village[42]

This location is known as a primary research location for those with an interest in Shaker history.

Shaker Museum and Library[43]

This library has a large collection of manuscripts, ephemera, and reference materials. While the materials are not available for interlibrary loan, the staff is helpful if you contact them by phone or email.

National Union Catalog of
Manuscript Collections (NUCMC)[44]

Search for Shaker manuscript collections in

various college and university libraries.

Western Reserve Historical Society[45]

This Ohio historical society contains microfilm records of Shaker membership files, manuscripts, and printed materials from all Shaker communities.

New York State Library[46]

One of the largest collections, this repository holds a vast collection of Shaker manuscripts, photographs, and more.

On-line Research: The Shakers

Websites

Cyndi's List: Shakers[47]

One of genealogy's go-to sites, Cyndi's List includes a large list of links with quite a few relating to specific Shaker communities.

ProQuest[48]

If your library has access to ProQuest, search

the database for resources such as the Shaker Collection, 1723-1952

Shaker Historical Society[49]

This society is home to a library, museum, historical programs, and more. If you are in the area, be sure to visit.

Shaker Heritage Society[50]

Visit for educational and historical programming and information.

Sabbathday Lake Shaker Village[51]

Located in Maine, this historical landmark has a full calendar of programming throughout the year that will help you understand how your Shaker relative lived.

Shaker Village of Pleasant Hill[52]

This fully-functioning historical landmark gives you opportunities to explore the historical museum, visit the farm, enjoy the preserve, and learn through living history programming to understand what life was like here when the Shakers lived in Kentucky.

Hancock Shaker Village[53]

This landmark is a living history village with costumed interpreters, activities, and more. It also includes 20 restored Shaker buildings!

Canterbury Shaker Village[54]

Visit and learn from a Shaker Village in New Hampshire. Living history programming, museum collections, and more are available for you to enjoy.

Message Boards

- **Shaker Message Board**[55] on Ancestry.com

PART FOUR: THE HUTTERITES

Introduction to The Hutterites

H utterites are an Anabaptist faith. They are considered a plain people and are also pacifists just as Quakers are. They live as a communal society that is typically closed to outside culture. The faith is of German origin, though migration locations include Moravia, Austria, Bohemia, Slovakia, Transylvania, and Romania before migrating to the United States and later Canada.

Church Structure

Because the Hutterite church is based on a colony living structure, the roles in the church reflect the colony's needs as well as the religious responsibilities of the church.

The minister, or Prediger, is the leader of the church. In addition to caring for the members of the church and providing traditional services, sermons, and support, he also works alongside a council of elected members. This council, called a Zullbrieder, is responsible for the day-to-day decisions within the colony. This council is made up of the minister, the colony and farm managers, and two to three men from the congregation who are in good standing. These positions are elected for life.

Records

Records include the colony's births, marriages, and deaths recorded along with family histories, though these are typically not accessible by the general public. The Family History Library in Salt Lake City, Utah, along with some societies, hold limited family histories in their catalogs. You may find records in the surrounding communities.

Research Tips

- Look at local genealogy resources for the area in which your family settled.
- South Dakota and Canadian records and local historical societies may contain family histories.
- Consider other Anabaptist resources such as

Mennonite as Hutterite histories may be included.

- Follow the migration trail and research immigration records including ship logs.

Time Line: The Hutterites

1528: The Hutterite community is established in Moravia under the leadership of Jacob Hutter.

1536: Jacob Hutter is burned at the stake as a heretic.

1770: Many Hutterites flee to Russian Ukraine.

1873: Hutterites first arrive in New York in July 1873 via passage from Russia. They then migrate to South

Dakota.

1918: Hutterite migration to Canada to protect their status as conscientious objectors during World War I.

Migration Patterns: The Hutterites

T he Hutterite church first appeared in Switzerland. Along the way, due to persecution in various areas of Europe, the Swiss Hutterites joined together with Anabaptists from areas with in Germany. Thanks to another wave of persecution, the Hutterites once again moved further east into Russia. A third wave a persecution brought our Hutterite ancestors into the United States and Canada. It's an interesting and sad history that takes them from country to country. I encourage you to read through the references listed in the **On-line Research** section, no matter how short.

A Quick Overview of Major Migration Patterns

- **1520s:** The early Hutterites moved throughout Switzerland into Moravia.

- **1530s:** Following a split in the church, migration took some families into South Germany through Austria.

- **1622:** Migration from Moravia to Slovakia begins.

- **1760s:** Colonies once again begin to migrate due to persecution. While some colonies settle in Romania, the majority continue to Ukraine.

- **1877:** The three major colonies migrate from Ukraine to America. These colonies form the beginning of the three major divisions in the church.

- **1918:** American Hutterites leave the country and settle in Canada due to their pacifist stance against the country's involvement in World War I.

Locations of Current Colonies

- Canada: Alberta, British Columbia, Manitoba, and Saskatchewan.
- United States: Minnesota, Montana, North Dakota, Oregon, South Dakota, and Washington.

Terminology: The Hutterites

H utterite communities speak an Upper German dialect called Hutterite German or Hutterisch. However, children are taught English as they are older. You can learn more about that at Hutterites.org[56].

Basic Terminology

Gebet: an evening church service

Ordnung: order

Prediger: pastor

Strof: punishment

Zullbrieder: The colony's council responsible for the day-to-day decisions within the community

Major Repositories: The Hutterites

T he Hutterite church is very private and isn't typically open to those outside the community. However, you may find private correspondence and personal papers in local and state level repositories such as universities, historical societies, and genealogical societies. Also check with Mennonite repositories as there may be Hutterite papers among their archives as well.

Repositories

North Dakota State University Library: Germans from Russia Collection[57]

Remember to follow your migration patterns. Many of our Hutterite ancestors were among the Germans that migrated through Ukraine into the United States. Ethnic collections and societies will likely contain some information on the families that immigrated during these times.

Mennonite Church USA[58]

This Mennonite Church repository also holds many records useful to those with Hutterite ancestors. Hint: Look through the Archival Finding Aids to locate materials such as personal papers, correspondence, and wartime diaries. Correspondence between churches shows the joint opinions they issued in regards to social issues of the day such as slavery.

Goshen College
Mennonite Historical Library[59]

As with the Mennonite Church USA Archives, the Goshen College library includes histories, personal papers, biographies, and other documents related to the Hutterite church. While it is a small portion of their holdings, it's worth looking into.

On-line Research: The Hutterites

Websites

Hutterian Brethren[60]

This website is a great primer for those new to the structure, history, and culture of the Hutterite church. This official site will give you a great education in an approachable way.

Global Anabaptist Mennonite Encyclopedia On-line: Hutterian Brethren[61]

This wiki site gives researchers an easy history of the church including information on the migrations, leaders, and events that occurred over the last five hundred years.

Hutterite Saskatchewan Genealogy Roots[62]

Saskatchewan GenWeb site hosts a long list of ethnic projects related to the area, including one for the Hutterite church. If you have Canadian ancestors in the area, you may want to check out their other resources as well.

The Federation of East European Family History Societies: Hutterite Genealogy Resources[63]

This is one of my favorite sites! Biographies, ship records, primers and more are presented for free. Check out the other resources available on the site for Eastern European ancestors.

Hutterites: A Selected Bibliography[64]

A short history with a selection of books to get you on your way. It's a quick start to an interesting topic.

The Hutterian Brethren: A History[65]

The University of Alberta provides a thorough history of the church including demographics and statistics. The sections on life within the colonies gives us a look at their education, leisure time, and more. While it is primarily about those living in Alberta, there are references to American colonies as well.

Hutterite Genealogy[66]

Don't let the plain appearance of this site fool you. The links provided will lead you to learn more about your ancestors in a variety of locations, stateside and abroad.

Hutterite Colonies: A list[67]

Alberta ancestors? This simple page is a list of the Hutterite colonies in which they may have lived.

Facebook Groups

Hutterites, Mennonites, & Amish: Unite[68]

A group for those in the churches or interested in knowing more about them, their culture or their history. It may be a good way to connect with someone within the community.

Message Boards

Although they are not specifically for Hutterite research, Ancestry.com hosts several message boards that may be helpful:

- **Prussian-Russian Mennonites**[69]
- **Canada's General Message Board**[70]
- **Switzerland's General Message Board**[71]

PART FIVE: FURTHER READING

Reading List

General Topics

Kraybill, Donald B. and Carl F. Bowman. On the Backroad to Heaven: Old Order Hutterites, Mennonites, Amish, and Brethren. Baltimore: The Johns Hopkins University Press. 2001.

Lehman, James O. and Steven M. Nolt. Mennonites, Amish, and the American Civil War. Baltimore: The Johns Hopkins University Press. 2007.

Amish

Beachy, Leroy. Unser Leit: The Story of the Amish. Millersburg: Goodly Heritage Books. 2011.

Wagler, Ira. Growing Up Amish: A Memoir. Carol Stream: Tyndale House Publishers, Inc. 2011.

Mennonite

Kroeker, Wally. An Introduction to the Russian Mennonites. Intercourse: Good Books. 2005.

Huebert, Helmut T. and William Schroeder. Mennonite Historical Atlas. Hillsboro: Springfield Publishers. 1996.

Huguenot

Chater, Kathy. Tracing Your Huguenot Ancestors: A Guide for Family Historians. South Yorkshire: Pen & Sword Family History. 2012.

Finnell, Arthur Louis. National Huguenot Society Bible Records. Baltimore: Genealogical Publishing Company. 1996.

Shaker

Bauer, Cheryl. The Shakers of Union Village. Charleston: Arcadia Publishing. 2007.

Stein, Stephen J. The Shaker Experience in America: A History of the United Society of Believers. New Haven: Yale University Press. 1992.

Hutterite

Kirkby, Mary-Ann. I Am Hutterite: The Fascinating True Story of a Young Women's Journey to Reclaim Her Heritage. Nashville: Thomas Nelson. 2010.

Stahl, Lisa Marie. My Hutterite Life. Helena: Farcountry Press. 2003.

Bonus: Learn through Video!

PBS Home Video, Ken Burns' America: The Shakers. 2004.

Using Google Books

I love Google Books! I use this site quite often when I'm looking for county histories. It's amazing to see the titles that pop up. Nothing is better (to me) than reading a book written by a local about the county during the time my family was there. It's also great for finding first-hand accounts and information on various groups or organizations. Google Books is plain and simple a handy tool for learning more about your plain ancestors.

Tips and Tricks

Free books do exist. When researching my own family, I've found that the majority of the titles in which my family appeared happened to be free. You may be tempted to order an expensive out of print or rare book, but give free eBooks a try. Search for those and you'll be surprised what you find!

Get creative on your searches. Search by the name alone, by the name + geographic region, by church name, and by family name.

Think differently. Spelling errors, regional differences, and historical variations exist. Try different phrases and spellings to widen your results. Don't forget that in the case of some churches like the Huguenots, you may want to search for the original French spelling of the surname as well as the Anglicized version.

Use your search options. Look for books listed as free ebooks. Some newer books may include samples and searches.

Get organized. Many genealogies and family histories exist in ebook form on Google Books. Use your Library Bookshelf to organize the results by surname, location, time period, etc.

Examples

Baird, Charles Washington. History of the Huguenot Emigration to America, Volume 1. New York: Dodd, Mead, & Company. 1883.

Hartzler, Jonas Smucker and Daniel Kauffman. Mennonite Church History. Scottdale: Mennonite Book and Tract Society. 1905.

Sears, Clara Endicott. Gleanings from Old Shaker Journals. Boston and New York: The Riverside Press Cambridge, Houghton Mifflin Company. 1916.

Researching Your Quaker Family History

A Quick & Easy Guide for Genealogists

Known for their passive stance against war, an involvement in social reform initiatives, and having a simple or "plain" appearance, the Quakers have been part of American history since before the formation of our country.

In *Researching Your Quaker Family History*, you will find tips, tricks, and information relating to the structure of the Society of Friends meetings, the records that they produced and how you can use them to learn more about your family. Additional resources include time lines, terminology lists, and resources for researching both on line and in repositories.

Researching Your Quaker Family History

can be found in paperback and for Kindle

on Amazon.com

Finding Eliza

*"It's just a little family history.
What could go wrong?"*

When Lizzie Clydell agreed to join her grandmother at the church's genealogy group meeting she expected nothing more than lemon squares and a few stories. Instead, an old diary leads Lizzie down a dusty road of lies, hidden family secrets, and a lynching that nearly destroyed her family.

Still strug-gling with the loss of her parents two decades ear-lier, Lizzie must con-front a painful past that others hoped was forgotten. Her journey becomes even more difficult as she realizes those around her may not be as they seem.

Reviews for *Finding Eliza*

"Not since Steel Magnolias has a group of southern belles been as strong, charming, and funny. Throw in a compelling mystery and poignant history, and you've got a can't-put-down, can't-miss hit."

"Stephanie nailed this story from beginning to end. Her writing sings and the story flows drawing you in and keeping you spellbound. I read straight through in less than 3 days because I simply couldn't put. it. down. I was lost in Lizzie's world of a young girl pushing back a deep hurt from years past, and her Grandmother and friends who loved her enough to help her face that hurt. Through the anguish experienced by her ancestors, who suffered through the deep darkness of a post-civil war era, Lizzie comes to understand her own loss, and ultimately, to embrace it."

"I felt like Lizzie, I was drawn to her great grandfather's diary, I couldn't stop reading. The worst part I was on the last two chapters and I just couldn't stay awake to find out how it ended. First thing I did was make a cup of coffee and finished the book this morning! What an amazing book! I can't imagine the emotions of finding out the history of one's past like this, and actually being there to see face the face the man responsible. I don't want to reveal too much in this review. But, please, read this book, it's amazing! It makes me want to dig into my family history."

"*Finding Eliza* by Stephanie Pitcher Fishman is

a heartwarming book that pulled me in quite quickly. Fishman's love of genealogy and history is quite evident and she provides unvarnished glimpses of the not too distant past in the American South. I finished the book with two strong messages in mind: We have much to learn from history, especially our personal history and forgiveness has the power to set us free as long as we remember to forgive ourselves as well."

Finding Eliza can be found for paperback and Kindle on Amazon.com.

Thank You

T hank you for purchasing this Quick & Easy Guide for Genealogists pocket guide. I hope that it has been a helpful resource in your family history research. I'd love to hear from you. If you'd like to share your research stories or ask me about something in this guide, please email me at: stephanie@stephaniefishman.com.

Check Out My Fiction

In addition to writing non-fiction, I love creating characters and story lines that speak to the heart of the reader. I'd love for you to sample my stories for free.

Get a free copy of Shutter Step, a short fiction anthology by five indie authors, for free when you sign up at my website. Each story will take you someplace different - in five minutes or less. It's perfect for slipping time in with a book during your busy day.

Visit my website to get your free copy: www.stephaniefishman.com/shutter-step

About the Author

I chase dead people. I've grown up hearing family stories all of my life. In 1998, I picked up a new hobby as a way to pass the time with my grandmother. I now perform genealogical research for clients as well. I love to discover and share the stories of our ancestors. The words found in documents like marriage records and newspaper articles tell the stories of our families. In addition to providing research services, I enjoy creating narratives of family stories for my relatives as well as the relatives of clients. I am also active as a presenter speaking to genealogy groups and societies on topics related to family history research.

I've been a freelance writer for several years writing mostly on the subject of family history for blogs, websites, and genealogy societies and publications. I've also been a ghostwriter for areas ranging from air conditioning to the food service industry. I've enjoyed writing about family history much more than Chinese food. I'm a 14-year veteran homeschool mom who tries her best to raise creative and curious kids. Two have survived into adulthood, so we can't be all that bad at it. The youngest is a triple threat: writer, musician, and artist. I'm hoping to work on a few projects with her in the future.

My favorite book will always be Rebecca by Daphne DuMaurier. I remember sitting in the classroom after school as my eighth grade English teacher introduced me to it. I had read everything on our list for that grade so she gave me her favorite titles to read instead. I also learned that at age thirteen I didn't enjoy Steinbeck but I loved Orwell.

During high school and college I bounced between creative and nonfiction writing with even a stint on a community college newspaper. I was just too nervous to tell anyone about it. Very few people read my words so it surprises me that my parents knew I wanted to be a writer before I was able to speak it aloud. As I got closer to a milestone year I decided to break out of my fear and start writing my books with the goal of sharing them with others. *Finding Eliza*, my first novel, was a fortieth birthday present to myself. I hope you've enjoyed it.

I'm in love with the Oxford Comma. I'm hopelessly addicted to having my heart ripped out by BBC dramas. I love to insert references to history, pop culture, and humor into my writing and conversation. I currently have purple hair. I believe Joss Whedon can strike creative lightning at whim.

Official Biography

Stephanie Pitcher Fishman is an author and professional genealogist specializing in Midwestern and Southeastern United States family history. In addition to the Quick & Easy Guide for Genealogists series, she is the author of four family history research guides in the Legacy QuickGuide series focusing on state-specific research techniques. She has also written articles and blog posts for websites such as Archives.com and is a co-founder of The In-Depth Genealogist. She is also an active member of the Ohio Genealogical Society volunteering by lecturing on topics such as Plain Religions, Quaker research, and introducing family history to children. Her first novel, Finding Eliza, was published in 2014. To learn more, visit: www.StephanieFishman.com.

Connect with Stephanie

Facebook:

www.facebook.com/StephaniePitcherFishman

Facebook Group:

www.facebook.com/groups/SPFforReaders

Twitter:

@stephpfishman

Pinterest:

www.pinterest.com/stephpfishman

Also by
Stephanie Pitcher Fishman

Fiction

Finding Eliza

Shutter Step

The Widow Teal: A serialized novel

Quick & Easy Guides
for Genealogists

Researching Your Quaker Family History

Researching the Plain Religions

Research Bundle: Quakers & Plain Religions

Researching Your Ancestors
Using the U.S. Census

Legacy Family Tree
QuickGuides Series

Ohio Genealogy

Georgia Genealogy

Alabama Genealogy

Florida Genealogy

Links

H ere you'll find all of the links to the websites listed in this guide. You can also find them on a special website just for you! Visit the special website listed below to have easy access to live links.

Website: http://www.stephaniefishman.com/rl-plain
Password: PLrel2015

The Amish & Mennonites

[1] http://bit.ly/1OZMqbk

[2] http://bit.ly/1kbT0hv

[3] http://bit.ly/1MtZlly

[4] http://bit.ly/1M2uz0M

[5] http://bit.ly/1GxIzQ9

[6] http://bit.ly/1OZMqYI

[7] http://bit.ly/1ijnL2W

[8] http://bit.ly/1KGurio

[9] http://bit.ly/1MtZCF8

[10] http://bit.ly/1XzGgA0

[11] http://bit.ly/1XzGh72

[12] http://bit.ly/1RC9lXz

[13] http://bit.ly/1WjtV0s

[14] http://bit.ly/1LCM06G

[15] http://bit.ly/1Wil3NX

[16] http://bit.ly/1M2uPgz

[17] http://bit.ly/1OZMuaT

[18] http://bit.ly/1jSkYzp

[19] http://bit.ly/1N9fITi

[20] http://bit.ly/1N9fJXs

[21] http://1.usa.gov/1GKtZ7J

[22] http://bit.ly/1jSl3TG

[23] http://on.fb.me/1PV6UBb

[24] http://on.fb.me/1MUELos

[25] http://bit.ly/1LYPwGH

[26] http://bit.ly/1GKulv1

[27] http://bit.ly/1kTgadc

The Huguenots

[28] http://bit.ly/1KGvK0A

[29] http://bit.ly/1PREFnU

[30] http://bit.ly/1LCMJVv

[31] http://bit.ly/1PREVU0

[32] http://bit.ly/1LCKMZi

[33] http://bit.ly/1Hcm4ed

[34] http://bit.ly/1kbWuRp

[35] http://bit.ly/1PRH165

[36] http://bit.ly/1PRH3uT

[37] http://bit.ly/1KGvK0A

[38] http://bit.ly/1jSmLoh

[39] http://on.fb.me/1P68dwx

[40] http://on.fb.me/1XzIoaW

[41] http://bit.ly/1NBLvL4

The Shakers

[42] http://bit.ly/1GKxye1

[43] http://bit.ly/1OZMzLY

[44] http://1.usa.gov/1Mu2lhF

[45] http://bit.ly/1XzJcg7

[46] http://bit.ly/1kTliOy

[47] http://bit.ly/1ReW2wq

---

[48] http://bit.ly/1PRIx8t

[49] http://bit.ly/1GKyC1j

[50] http://bit.ly/1ijtxSe

[51] http://bit.ly/1GKxye1

[52] http://bit.ly/1LYQgvq

[53] http://bit.ly/1Wio7cL

[54] http://bit.ly/1kbZPzD

[55] http://bit.ly/1ReWtqG

The Hutterites

[56] http://bit.ly/1PRIUjo

[57] http://bit.ly/1O8wS4T

[58] http://bit.ly/1kbT0hv

[59] http://bit.ly/1M2uz0M

[60] http://bit.ly/1XzTlJN

[61] http://bit.ly/1KGEHHq

[62] http://bit.ly/1Mubg2E

[63] http://bit.ly/1HcARWf

[64] http://bit.ly/1GxNKzq

[65] http://bit.ly/1M2zPlk

[66] http://bit.ly/1Rf1BuI

[67] http://bit.ly/1LYSo6h

[68] http://on.fb.me/1XzUIYY

[69] http://bit.ly/1kTgadc

[70] http://bit.ly/1WjAosi

[71] http://bit.ly/1OZMWWT